Table Of Contents

Introduction

Why unlocking your creative spirit is important for renewed faith

In today's fast-paced and technology-driven world, we often lose touch with our creative spirit. As Christians, we are called to be creative and use our talents to glorify God. However, when we become too focused on our daily routines and responsibilities, we forget to tap into our creative side. This is why unlocking your creative spirit is essential for renewed faith.

When we engage in creative activities, we are opening ourselves up to new experiences and perspectives. This can help us see God's work in new ways and deepen our relationship with Him. For example, through artistic Bible study methods, we can use our creativity to explore and interpret scripture in unique and meaningful ways. We can also use drama and storytelling in our sermons to convey God's messages in a more engaging and memorable way.

Christian mindfulness and meditation also allow us to tap into our creative spirit and connect with God on a deeper level. Through these practices, we can quiet our minds and focus on our faith, opening ourselves up to new insights and revelations. Writing and journaling for faith exploration is another effective way to unlock our creativity and deepen our relationship with God. By reflecting on our thoughts and experiences, we can gain new perspectives and insights into our faith.

Finally, healing through the arts is an important aspect of unlocking our creative spirit. When we engage in creative activities such as painting, music, or dance, we are able to express ourselves in ways that words cannot. This can help us process and heal from past wounds and traumas, and deepen our faith in the process.

In conclusion, unlocking your creative spirit is essential for renewed faith. By engaging in creative activities such as artistic Bible study methods, drama and storytelling in sermons, Christian mindfulness and meditation, writing and journaling for faith exploration, and healing through the arts, we can deepen our relationship with God and gain new insights into our faith. So, let us all take the time to tap into our creative spirit and use our talents to glorify God.

The benefits of incorporating creative practices into your spiritual life

Creativity is a vital part of the human experience. It is a gift that we all possess and can use to express ourselves in unique and beautiful ways. Incorporating creative practices into your spiritual life can help you connect with your Creator in deeper and more meaningful ways. In this subchapter, we will explore the benefits of incorporating creative practices into your spiritual life.

Right Brained Christianity

Right-brained Christianity is a way of approaching spirituality through creative and intuitive processes. It encourages us to use our imagination and creativity to connect with God in new and exciting ways. By engaging our right-brain, we can move beyond traditional methods of prayer and worship to experience God in a more personal and meaningful way.

Artistic Bible Study Methods

Artistic Bible study methods involve using our creativity to explore the Scriptures. This can include drawing, painting, or even creating collages that reflect our understanding of the text. By engaging with the Bible in this way, we can gain new insights and deeper understanding of God's Word.

Drama and Storytelling in Sermons

Drama and storytelling are powerful tools that can be used to communicate the message of the Bible in a fresh and engaging way. Through drama and storytelling, we can bring the stories of the Bible to life and help our audience connect with the message on a deeper level.

Christian Mindfulness and Meditation

Christian mindfulness and meditation involve using our breath and our senses to connect with God. By being still and quiet before God, we can open ourselves up to His presence and allow Him to speak to us in new and profound ways.

Writing and Journaling for Faith Exploration

Writing and journaling can be powerful tools for exploring our faith. By putting our thoughts and feelings down on paper, we can gain new insights into our relationship with God and discover new ways of connecting with Him.

Healing Through the Arts

The arts have the power to heal and restore us. Through music, dance, and other creative practices, we can express our emotions and find healing for our wounds. By incorporating these practices into our spiritual life, we can experience the transformative power of God's love in new and profound ways. Psalm 149:3 "Let them praise His name with dancing; Let them sing praises to Him with timbrel and lyre."

Incorporating creative practices into your spiritual life can help you connect with your Creator in deeper and more meaningful ways. Whether you are exploring right-brained Christianity, using artistic Bible study methods, or finding healing through the arts, there are countless ways to tap into your creative spirit and deepen your relationship with God. So, embrace your creativity and let it lead you into a deeper understanding of God's love and grace. Psalm 51:10 "Create in me a clean heart, O God; and renew a right spirit within me."

Who this book is for and what it will cover

Who this book is for and what it will cover

If you are someone who has lost touch with your Creator and yearns to renew your communication with Him, then this book is for you. It is for those who feel disconnected from their faith and are looking for ways to reconnect with God. Whether you are an artist, writer, or simply someone seeking a different approach to your faith, this book will offer you insights, tools, and techniques to unlock your creative spirit and rekindle your relationship with God. Psalm 139: 13-14 "and he has filled him with the Spirit of God, with wisdom, with understanding, with knowledge and with all kinds of skills—to make artistic designs for work in gold, silver and bronze, to cut and set stones, to work in wood and to engage in all kinds of artistic crafts."

The book is geared towards those who are interested in Right-Brained Christianity, which is an approach that focuses on using the creative and intuitive side of the brain to connect with God. It is a way of embracing your creativity and using it as a means of deepening your faith. The book will also cover Artistic Bible Study Methods, which will show you how to use art and creative expression as a way of studying the Bible and understanding its message.

Drama and Storytelling in Sermons is another topic that will be covered in the book. It is a powerful way of engaging your audience and helping them to connect with the message of your sermon. You will learn how to use drama and storytelling to bring the Bible to life and make it relevant to your audience.

Christian Mindfulness and Meditation is another area that will be explored in the book. You will learn how to use mindfulness and meditation as a way of deepening your connection with God and developing a more intimate relationship with Him. You will also learn how to use Writing and Journaling for Faith Exploration, which is a powerful tool for self-reflection and personal growth.

Finally, the book will cover Healing through the Arts, which is an approach that uses art and creativity as a means of healing emotional wounds and finding spiritual renewal. You will learn how to use art, writing, and other creative expressions as a way of working through your pain and finding healing. Ephesians 5:19 Speaking to yourselves in psalms and hymns and spiritual songs, singing and making melody in your heart to the Lord"

In summary, this book is for those who are seeking a new approach to their faith and are interested in using their creativity as a means of deepening their relationship with God. It will cover a range of topics, from Right-Brained Christianity and Artistic Bible Study Methods to Drama and Storytelling in Sermons, Christian Mindfulness and Meditation, Writing and Journaling for Faith Exploration, and Healing through the Arts. By the end of the book, you will have a toolkit of creative techniques and spiritual practices that will help you to reconnect with God and unlock your creative spirit.

Understanding Right-Brained Christianity

The difference between left-brained and right-brained thinking

The difference between left-brained and right-brained thinking is a concept that has been explored by scientists and psychologists for decades. It is believed that the brain is divided into two hemispheres, each with its unique characteristics and functions. The left hemisphere is associated with analytical thinking, logic, language, and mathematics, while the right hemisphere is associated with creativity, intuition, emotions, and visualization.

Right-brained Christianity is a way of approaching faith from a creative and intuitive perspective. It is about tapping into the right hemisphere of the brain to connect with God and experience spirituality in a more holistic and meaningful way. By understanding the difference between left-brained and right-brained thinking, we can learn to balance our cognitive and creative abilities and cultivate a deeper relationship with our Creator.

Artistic Bible study methods are one way to tap into our right-brained thinking and connect with God on a deeper level. Using visual aids, music, drama, and storytelling, we can explore the scriptures in a more creative and engaging way. By incorporating our senses and emotions, we can gain a deeper understanding of God's word and develop a more personal relationship with Him.

Drama and storytelling in sermons are also effective ways to engage our right-brained thinking and communicate the message of the gospel in a more impactful way. By using characters, plot, and dialogue, we can bring the stories of the Bible to life and help our audience connect with the message on a deeper level.

Christian mindfulness and meditation are practices that can help us tap into our right-brained thinking and cultivate a deeper sense of peace and connection with God. By focusing on our breath, our senses, and our emotions, we can quiet our minds and open ourselves up to the presence of God.

Writing and journaling for faith exploration are also powerful tools for tapping into our right-brained thinking and exploring our relationship with God. By expressing our thoughts and feelings on paper, we can gain a deeper understanding of ourselves and our spirituality, and connect with God in a more personal and meaningful way. Isaiah 30:8 ""Go now, and write it down on a tablet in their presence, inscribing it in a book, so that for times to come it may be an everlasting witness."

Finally, healing through the arts is a powerful way to tap into our right-brained thinking and find healing and renewal in our faith. Whether it's through music, art, dance, or theater, we can use the creative arts to express our emotions, connect with God, and find healing and wholeness in our lives.

In conclusion, understanding the difference between left-brained and right-brained thinking is essential for unlocking our creative spirit and renewing our faith. By tapping into our right-brained thinking and incorporating creative practices into our spiritual lives, we can cultivate a deeper relationship with God and experience a more holistic and meaningful faith.

How right-brained Christianity can enhance your faith

How right brained Christianity can enhance your faith

Many Christians approach their faith from a left-brained perspective: logical, rational, and analytical. While this approach is valuable, it often misses out on the emotional and imaginative aspects of faith that can be accessed through the right brain. Right-brained Christianity involves engaging with God and the

Bible through creative practices like art, drama, storytelling, mindfulness, meditation, writing, and journaling.

When we engage with our faith through creative practices, we open ourselves up to a deeper understanding of God and his word. Artistic Bible study methods, for example, invite us to engage with scripture in a visual and tactile way. We can paint or draw scenes from the Bible, create collages of verses that resonate with us, or even use coloring books to meditate on the word of God. By engaging with the Bible in this way, we tap into our intuition and imagination, allowing the Holy Spirit to speak to us in new and profound ways.

Drama and storytelling in sermons can also bring the Bible to life in a way that engages both the left and right sides of our brain. When pastors use drama or storytelling to illustrate biblical truths, we are able to connect with the message on an emotional level, making it more memorable and impactful. By engaging with our faith in this way, we are able to internalize the message and apply it to our lives more effectively.

Christian mindfulness and meditation practices can also enhance our faith by helping us connect with God in the present moment. When we practice mindfulness, we are able to quiet our minds and focus on the present moment, allowing us to become more aware of God's presence in our lives. This can be done through guided meditations, prayer walks, or simply sitting in silence and focusing on our breath.

Writing and journaling for faith exploration can also be a powerful tool for deepening our relationship with God. By putting our thoughts and feelings onto paper, we are able to process our emotions and connect with God in a more intimate way. We can write prayers, meditations, or reflections on scripture, allowing us to explore our faith in a more personal and meaningful way.

Finally, healing through the arts can be a powerful way to connect with God and find healing for our emotional wounds. When we engage with music, dance, or other forms of artistic expression, we are able to tap into our emotions and connect with God in a way that can bring deep healing and restoration.

In conclusion, right-brained Christianity offers a rich and meaningful way to engage with our faith. By incorporating creative practices into our spiritual lives, we can deepen our relationship with God and find new and transformative ways to connect with the Bible and our Creator.

Incorporating creativity into your relationship with God

Incorporating creativity into your relationship with God can be a powerful way to renew your communication with Him. Many people find that traditional methods of prayer and worship can become stale over time, but incorporating creativity into your spiritual practices can help you to connect with God in a fresh and dynamic way.

One way to incorporate creativity into your relationship with God is through artistic Bible study methods. Instead of simply reading and analyzing scripture, try engaging with it through art. This might involve creating visual art, such as painting or drawing, that represents your interpretation of a particular passage. Alternatively, you could try writing poetry or composing a song inspired by a particular verse or story.

Drama and storytelling can also be powerful tools for connecting with God. Consider incorporating these elements into your sermons or personal prayer time. This might involve acting out a particular story or parable, or simply using dramatic storytelling techniques to bring scripture to life.

Christian mindfulness and meditation can also be enhanced through creativity. Try incorporating visual or auditory elements into your meditation practice, such as focusing on a particular image or sound. You might also try incorporating movement, such as walking or dancing, into your meditation practice.

Writing and journaling can be powerful tools for exploring your faith and deepening your relationship with God. Consider keeping a spiritual journal, where you can reflect on your experiences, insights, and prayers. You might also try writing prayers, poems, or other creative expressions of your faith.

Finally, the arts can be a powerful tool for healing and renewal. Consider incorporating music, dance, or other art forms into your spiritual practices as a way to connect with God and experience His healing presence. Ephesians 2:10 For we are His workmanship, created in Christ Jesus for good works, which God prepared beforehand so that we would walk in them."

Incorporating creativity into your relationship with God can be a powerful way to renew your communication with Him. Whether through artistic Bible study methods, drama and storytelling, Christian mindfulness and meditation, writing and journaling, or healing through the arts, there are many ways to connect with God in a creative and dynamic way. By exploring these methods, you can deepen your relationship with God and experience renewed faith and spiritual vitality.

Artistic Bible Study Methods

Using art and creative expression to study and understand scripture

Using art and creative expression to study and understand scripture is an effective way to connect with God and renew your communication with Him. This approach is known as Right-Brained Christianity, which emphasizes the use of creativity and imagination to deepen your understanding of the Bible.

Artistic Bible Study methods are a great way to engage with scripture in a more creative and interactive way. These methods include visual journaling, Bible journaling, and Bible art journaling. Visual journaling involves using images, colors, and collage to express your thoughts and feelings about a particular passage of scripture. Bible journaling involves writing down your reflections and insights in a journal alongside the text of the Bible. Bible art journaling involves combining art and writing to create a visual representation of your understanding of a particular passage.

Drama and storytelling are also effective tools for communicating the message of the Bible. Sermons can be enhanced by incorporating drama and storytelling to bring the message to life for the congregation. This approach can also be used in small group settings to create a more interactive and engaging Bible study experience.

Christian Mindfulness and Meditation is another way to connect with God through art and creative expression. This approach involves using art to focus your mind and deepen your spiritual practice. Through Christian mindfulness and meditation, you can explore your faith in a more contemplative way, allowing you to connect with God on a deeper level.

Writing and journaling are also effective ways to explore your faith and deepen your relationship with God. Writing and journaling can help you process your thoughts and emotions, providing a space to reflect on your spiritual journey. By writing down your thoughts and feelings, you can gain a deeper understanding of yourself and your relationship with God.

Finally, Healing Through the Arts is a powerful approach to connecting with God and finding emotional and spiritual healing. Through music, dance, and other forms of creative expression, you can explore your emotions and connect with God in a more profound way. This approach can be especially helpful for those who have experienced trauma or emotional pain.

In summary, using art and creative expression to study and understand scripture is an effective way to connect with God and deepen your spiritual practice. Whether through artistic Bible study methods, drama and storytelling, Christian mindfulness and meditation, writing and journaling, or healing through the arts, there are many ways to use creativity to connect with God and renew your communication with Him.

Techniques for incorporating art into your Bible study

The Bible is a work of art in itself, but there are many ways to bring more creativity and beauty into your study of scripture. Here are some techniques for incorporating art into your Bible study:

1. Bible Journaling: Bible journaling is a creative way to engage with scripture by adding art, handwriting, and even personal reflections to the pages of your Bible. It can be done with simple supplies like pens, markers, and stickers, or with more elaborate techniques like watercolor painting. Bible journaling helps to bring the words of the Bible to life and makes it easier to remember key verses.

2. Visual Art: Visual art can be used to illustrate the themes and stories of the Bible. This can be done through painting, drawing, or even sculpture. By creating art inspired by scripture, you can deepen your understanding of the text and connect with it in a more personal way.

3. Drama and Storytelling: Drama and storytelling can be powerful ways to bring the stories of the Bible to life. By acting out scenes or telling stories with vivid detail, you can help others to better understand the meaning behind the words. This technique can be used in sermons, Bible studies, or even in personal reflection.

4. Christian Mindfulness and Meditation: Christian mindfulness and meditation can help you to connect with God in a deeper way. By focusing on the present moment and opening your heart to the divine, you can cultivate a sense of peace and connection with the Creator. Mindfulness practices like breathing exercises and prayer can be incorporated into your Bible study to help you stay focused and centered.

5. Writing and Journaling: Writing and journaling can be powerful tools for exploring your faith. By reflecting on your experiences with God and your own spiritual journey, you can gain insights and deepen your connection with the divine. Writing can also help you to process difficult emotions and find healing through the arts.

6. Healing Through the Arts: The arts can be a powerful tool for healing and restoration. By engaging in creative activities like painting, music, or dance, you can express your emotions and find new ways to connect with God. The arts can also help you to connect with others who share your faith and find support and community through shared experiences.

These techniques for incorporating art into your Bible study can help you to deepen your connection with God and find new ways to express your faith. Whether you are a seasoned artist or a beginner, there are many ways to use the arts to enhance your spiritual practice and find renewed faith in the Creator.

The benefits of artistic Bible study

The Bible is a book that has inspired countless works of art, from paintings to sculptures to music. It is a rich source of inspiration for artistic expression and can be used as a tool for spiritual growth and renewal. Artistic Bible study is a way of exploring the Bible through creative expression, allowing individuals to connect with God in a deeper way.

One of the benefits of artistic Bible study is that it engages the right side of the brain. The right side of the brain is associated with creativity, intuition, and imagination. By using art to study the Bible, individuals can tap into this part of their brain and connect with God in a more holistic way. This can lead to a deeper understanding of the Bible and a more profound spiritual experience.

Artistic Bible study methods can take many forms, from drawing and painting to collage and mixed media. By using different materials and techniques, individuals can explore the Bible in a visual and tactile way. This can help to bring the stories and teachings of the Bible to life and make them more meaningful.

Drama and storytelling in sermons are also powerful tools for artistic Bible study. By using drama and storytelling to convey the lessons of the Bible, individuals can connect with the stories on a deeper level. This can help to make the Bible more relevant to daily life and inspire individuals to live out their faith.

Christian mindfulness and meditation can also be incorporated into artistic Bible study. By using art as a form of meditation, individuals can quiet their minds and focus on God. This can lead to a deeper sense of peace and a greater connection with the divine.

Writing and journaling for faith exploration is another way to incorporate artistic Bible study into daily life. By using writing as a tool for reflection and exploration, individuals can deepen their understanding of the Bible and their relationship with God.

Finally, healing through the arts can be a powerful way to use artistic Bible study to overcome emotional pain and trauma. By using art to express emotions and experiences related to faith, individuals can find healing and renewal.

Overall, artistic Bible study is a powerful tool for those seeking to renew their communication with God. It engages the right side of the brain, brings the Bible to life, and can lead to a deeper spiritual experience. Whether through drawing, drama, writing, or other forms of artistic expression, individuals can use art to connect with God and renew their faith.

Drama and Storytelling in Sermons

How drama and storytelling can enhance your sermons

As a pastor or preacher, it can be challenging to keep your congregation engaged and attentive during sermons. One way to enhance your sermons and keep your audience captivated is through the use of drama and storytelling.

Drama and storytelling have been used for centuries to convey important messages and teachings. By incorporating these elements into your sermons, you can bring your message to life and make it more relatable and memorable to your congregation.

One of the benefits of using drama and storytelling in your sermons is that it can help you connect with your audience on a deeper emotional level. When people are emotionally invested in a story, they are more likely to remember it and apply the lessons learned to their own lives.

Another benefit is that drama and storytelling can help you illustrate complex theological concepts and make them more accessible to your congregation. By using relatable characters and situations, you can help your audience understand difficult concepts in a way that is easy to comprehend.

Additionally, drama and storytelling can help you create a more dynamic and engaging worship experience. By incorporating elements of drama and storytelling into your sermons, you can create a more interactive and participatory environment that encourages your congregation to actively engage with your message.

There are many different ways to incorporate drama and storytelling into your sermons. You could use skits or plays to illustrate biblical stories or parables, or you could use personal anecdotes or stories to connect with your audience on a more personal level.

Overall, drama and storytelling can be powerful tools for enhancing your sermons and helping you connect with your congregation on a deeper level. By incorporating these elements into your worship services, you can create a more engaging and meaningful experience for your congregation and help them renew their communication with their Creator.

Techniques for incorporating drama and storytelling into your sermons

One of the most effective ways to connect with an audience during a sermon is through storytelling. Jesus himself often used parables and stories to illustrate his teachings. Incorporating drama and storytelling into your sermons can help bring the Bible to life for your congregation and make the message more relatable.

Here are some techniques for incorporating drama and storytelling into your sermons:

1. Use visual aids

Visual aids can help bring your story to life and make it more engaging for your audience. Consider using props, images, or video to illustrate your message.

2. Use character voices

Using different voices for different characters can help your audience better understand the story and connect with the characters. It can also make the story more entertaining.

3. Use humor

Humor can help lighten the mood and make the message more relatable. It can also help your audience remember the message long after the sermon is over.

4. Use real-life examples

Using real-life examples can help your audience connect with the message and apply it to their own lives. It can also make the message more relevant and relatable.

5. Use interactive elements

Incorporating interactive elements, such as role-playing or audience participation, can help your audience engage with the message and make it more memorable.

By incorporating these techniques into your sermons, you can create a more engaging and memorable experience for your congregation. This can help renew their communication with God and deepen their faith. Remember, the key is to make the message relatable and relevant to your audience.

The benefits of using drama and storytelling in your sermons

As a pastor or preacher, one of the most important aspects of your role is to connect with your congregation and to help them understand and live out the teachings of the Bible. However, this can be a challenge in today's fast-paced and distracted world. That's where drama and storytelling can come in. By incorporating these creative techniques into your sermons, you can engage your audience on a deeper level and help them to connect with the message in a more meaningful way.

One of the key benefits of using drama and storytelling in your sermons is that it can help to make the message more memorable. When people hear a story or see a dramatic scene acted out, they are more likely to remember the key points of the message than if you simply lecture to them. This can be especially helpful for those who are more visually-oriented or who struggle with traditional learning methods.

Another benefit of using drama and storytelling in your sermons is that it can help to create a sense of community among your congregation. When people come together to act out a scene or to listen to a story, they are participating in a shared experience that can help to build connections and foster a sense of belonging. This can be especially important for those who are feeling disconnected from their Creator or who are struggling with loneliness or isolation.

In addition to these benefits, drama and storytelling can also be powerful tools for healing and personal growth. By exploring biblical stories and characters through drama or writing exercises, individuals can gain new insights into their own lives and experiences. This can help to promote self-awareness, empathy, and compassion, all of which are key components of a healthy and fulfilling spiritual life.

Overall, incorporating drama and storytelling into your sermons can be a powerful way to connect with your congregation and to help them deepen their faith and understanding of the Bible. Whether you're using these techniques to help people remember key points of the message, to foster community, or to promote personal growth and healing, you're sure to find that they are a valuable addition to your creative toolkit.

Christian Mindfulness and Meditation

Understanding the importance of mindfulness and meditation in Christianity

Christianity is a religion that offers a deep sense of peace and purpose to its followers. Many people who have lost touch with their Creator often seek to renew their communication with Him. One powerful tool for achieving this is through the practice of mindfulness and meditation.

Mindfulness and meditation are ancient practices that have been used by many religious and spiritual traditions for centuries. In Christianity, these practices can help believers connect more deeply with their faith and with God. By practicing mindfulness and meditation, Christians can quiet their minds and hearts, allowing them to be more receptive to God's presence and guidance.

Mindfulness is a state of being fully present and aware of what is happening in the moment, without judgment or distraction. It is a practice of paying attention to one's thoughts, feelings, and surroundings without getting caught up in them. This practice can help Christians to become more aware of the presence of God in their lives, and to be more intentional about their spiritual practices.

Meditation, on the other hand, is a more focused practice of quieting the mind and entering into a state of deep reflection or prayer. It often involves the use of breathing techniques, mantras, or visualizations to help bring the mind into a state of stillness and concentration. This practice can help Christians to connect more deeply with God and to gain insight and wisdom from their spiritual experiences.

Both mindfulness and meditation can be practiced in a variety of ways, including through prayer, scripture reading, and contemplative practices such as walking or gardening. They can also be incorporated into artistic Bible study methods, drama and storytelling in sermons, writing and journaling for faith exploration, and healing through the arts.

In conclusion, the practice of mindfulness and meditation can be a powerful tool for Christians seeking to deepen their connection with God. By quieting the mind and opening the heart, these practices can help believers to become more aware of God's presence and to experience a deeper sense of peace and purpose in their spiritual lives.

Techniques for incorporating mindfulness and meditation into your spiritual life

As a Christian, you may feel that you have lost touch with your Creator, and that your faith has become stale or routine. One way to renew your communication with God is to incorporate mindfulness and meditation into your spiritual life.

Mindfulness is the practice of being present in the moment, and focusing your attention on your thoughts, feelings, and surroundings. Meditation is the practice of quieting your mind and focusing on a particular thought or object. Both practices can help you connect with God on a deeper level, and can enhance your spiritual life in many ways.

Here are some techniques for incorporating mindfulness and meditation into your spiritual life:

1. Set aside time for quiet reflection each day. You may want to start with just a few minutes each day, and gradually increase the time as you become more comfortable with the practice.

2. Choose a quiet, peaceful place where you can meditate and reflect without distractions. This might be a quiet room in your home, a peaceful outdoor space, or a church or other sacred space.

3. Use breathing exercises to help you focus your mind and calm your body. Breathe deeply and slowly, focusing on the sensation of the air moving in and out of your body.

4. Use guided meditations or mindfulness exercises to help you focus your thoughts and connect with God. There are many resources available online or in books that can help guide you through these practices.

5. Incorporate creativity into your mindfulness and meditation practices. For example, you might try journaling, drawing, or painting as a way to express your thoughts and feelings.

6. Finally, be patient and persistent. Mindfulness and meditation are skills that take time to develop, and it may take some time before you begin to see the benefits of these practices in your spiritual life. But with patience and persistence, you can develop a deeper connection with God and renew your communication with Him.

The benefits of Christian mindfulness and meditation

The practice of mindfulness and meditation has been around for centuries, but it has only recently gained popularity in Christian circles. The benefits of Christian mindfulness and meditation are numerous and can help you renew your communication with God.

One of the main benefits of Christian mindfulness and meditation is that it helps you develop a deeper relationship with God. When you take the time to quiet your mind and focus on God, you become more aware of His presence in your life. This awareness can help you feel more connected to God and more at peace with yourself and the world around you.

Another benefit of Christian mindfulness and meditation is that it can help you reduce stress and anxiety. When you are constantly worried or stressed, it can be difficult to hear God's voice and feel His presence in your life. By taking the time to quiet your mind and focus on God, you can reduce your stress levels and open yourself up to His guidance and wisdom.

Christian mindfulness and meditation can also help you improve your mental and emotional well-being. When you focus on God and His love for you, you can let go of negative thoughts and emotions that may be holding you back. This can help you feel more confident, happy, and fulfilled in your life.

If you are struggling to renew your communication with God, Christian mindfulness and meditation can be a powerful tool to help you reconnect with your Creator. By taking the time to quiet your mind and focus on God, you can deepen your relationship with Him and experience the many benefits of a closer walk with God.

In conclusion, Christian mindfulness and meditation are powerful tools that can help you renew your communication with God, reduce stress and anxiety, improve your mental and emotional well-being, and deepen your relationship with your Creator. Whether you are an artist, writer, or storyteller, incorporating these practices into your daily life can help you unlock your creative spirit and experience a renewed sense of faith and purpose in your life.

Writing and Journaling for Faith Exploration

How writing and journaling can help you explore and deepen your faith

Writing and journaling are powerful tools that can help you explore and deepen your faith. Whether you are a seasoned believer or someone who has lost touch with their Creator, writing and journaling can help you renew your communication with Him.

One of the main benefits of writing and journaling is that it allows you to express your thoughts and feelings in a safe and non-judgmental way. When you write, you can be completely honest and vulnerable with yourself and with God. You can explore your doubts, fears, hopes, and dreams, and you can ask Him for guidance and wisdom.

Writing and journaling can also help you connect with your inner voice and intuition. Sometimes, we get so caught up in our busy lives that we forget to listen to our own hearts and souls. When you write, you can tap into your subconscious mind and access your deepest thoughts and feelings. You can also connect with God's voice and receive His messages and inspirations.

Another benefit of writing and journaling is that it helps you gain clarity and perspective. When you put your thoughts and feelings on paper, you can see them more clearly and objectively. You can also organize your ideas and prioritize your goals. This can help you make better decisions and take action towards your dreams.

Writing and journaling can also be a form of self-care and healing. When you write, you release pent-up emotions and negative thoughts. This can help you reduce stress, anxiety, and depression. You can also use writing and journaling to process past traumas and wounds. This can help you heal and move forward in your life and faith.

In conclusion, writing and journaling are powerful tools that can help you explore and deepen your faith. They can help you express your thoughts and feelings, connect with your inner voice and intuition, gain clarity and perspective, and promote self-care and healing. If you want to renew your communication with God and unlock your creative spirit, start writing and journaling today.

Techniques for incorporating writing and journaling into your spiritual life

The art of writing and journaling is a powerful tool to aid in spiritual growth and exploration. For those seeking to renew their communication with their Creator, incorporating writing and journaling into their spiritual life can help them to discover and explore their faith in new ways.

One technique for incorporating writing and journaling into your spiritual life is to set aside time each day for reflection and contemplation. This could be in the form of a daily devotion or meditation, where you take time to reflect on your faith and connect with your Creator. During this time, you can write down your thoughts, prayers, and insights, allowing them to flow freely and unhindered.

Another technique is to use writing and journaling as a tool for self-discovery. By exploring your thoughts and feelings through writing, you can gain a deeper understanding of yourself and your relationship with God. This can involve writing about your struggles, fears, and doubts, as well as your hopes, dreams, and aspirations. By doing so, you can uncover new insights and perspectives, and develop a deeper sense of trust and faith in your Creator.

Writing and journaling can also be used as a powerful tool for healing and transformation. By exploring your emotions and experiences through writing, you can gain a new perspective on your life and find healing and wholeness in your faith. This could involve writing about past traumas or struggles, as well as your current challenges and obstacles. By doing so, you can release negative emotions, gain clarity and insight, and move forward in your spiritual journey with renewed strength and vigor.

Whether you are looking to renew your communication with your Creator, explore your faith in new ways, or find healing and transformation through the arts, incorporating writing and journaling into your spiritual life can be a powerful and transformative practice. By taking time each day to reflect, explore, and connect with your Creator through writing, you can unlock your creative spirit and discover new depths of faith, hope, and love.

The benefits of writing and journaling for faith exploration

Writing and journaling can be incredibly beneficial for those who are looking to explore their faith and reconnect with their Creator. These activities can help individuals to gain a deeper understanding of themselves, their beliefs, and their relationship with God.

One of the primary benefits of writing and journaling is that it allows individuals to express their thoughts and emotions in a safe and private space. This can be especially helpful for those who may feel uncomfortable discussing their faith with others or who may be struggling to articulate their feelings. By putting their thoughts down on paper, individuals can gain clarity and insight into their beliefs and experiences.

In addition to being a tool for self-reflection, writing and journaling can also be a way to explore and deepen one's understanding of the Bible and other spiritual texts. By writing about specific passages or verses, individuals can gain new insights and perspectives that they may not have otherwise considered. This can help to deepen their faith and provide a greater sense of connection to the divine.

Writing and journaling can also be a way to cultivate gratitude and mindfulness in one's spiritual practice. By focusing on the blessings and experiences that bring joy and meaning to our lives, we can develop a greater appreciation for the beauty and wonder of the world around us. This can help to foster a sense of peace and contentment, even in the midst of difficult circumstances.

Finally, writing and journaling can be a powerful tool for healing and transformation. By exploring our thoughts and feelings in a safe and supportive environment, we can work through emotional wounds and traumas, and find a greater sense of wholeness and healing. Through writing and journaling, we can tap into the transformative power of the creative process and discover new depths of faith and spiritual connection.

In conclusion, for those who have lost touch with their Creator and want to renew their communication with Him, writing and journaling can be a powerful tool for exploring and deepening their faith. Whether through self-reflection, Bible study, gratitude practice, or healing and transformation, these activities can help individuals to cultivate a richer, more meaningful spiritual life.

Healing Through the Arts

Understanding how the arts can be used for healing and restoration

Understanding how the arts can be used for healing and restoration is critical for anyone who wants to renew their communication with God. Artistic expressions have always been an integral part of human history, and they have played a significant role in various cultures and religions throughout the world. In recent times, the use of art for healing and restoration has received more attention, and researchers have discovered that the arts can be a powerful tool in facilitating spiritual and emotional healing.

Right-brained Christianity is an approach that recognizes the importance of creative expression in fostering spiritual growth and renewal. Artistic Bible study methods, drama, and storytelling in sermons are just some of the ways that right-brained Christianity can be incorporated into your spiritual practice. These methods allow you to engage with the Bible in a more creative and intuitive way, enabling you to connect with God on a deeper level.

Christian mindfulness and meditation are other powerful tools for spiritual renewal. The practice of mindfulness involves being fully present in the moment, observing your thoughts and feelings without judgment, and cultivating a sense of inner calm and peace. Christian meditation involves focusing your thoughts on God, connecting with His presence, and allowing His love and grace to fill your heart.

Writing and journaling for faith exploration are also powerful tools for spiritual growth and renewal. Writing allows you to express your thoughts and feelings in a structured and organized way, providing clarity and insight into your spiritual journey. Journaling, on the other hand, is a more personal and introspective form of writing, allowing you to explore your thoughts and feelings in a more unstructured and creative way.

Lastly, healing through the arts is a powerful form of therapy that has been used for centuries. Art therapy, music therapy, dance therapy, and other forms of creative expression have been shown to be effective in treating a wide range of emotional and psychological issues, including depression, anxiety, trauma, and addiction.

In conclusion, understanding how the arts can be used for healing and restoration is essential for anyone who wants to renew their communication with God. Incorporating right-brained Christianity, artistic Bible study methods, drama and storytelling in sermons, Christian mindfulness and meditation, writing and journaling for faith exploration, and healing through the arts into your spiritual practice can provide a powerful and transformative experience that can help you connect with God on a deeper level.

Techniques for incorporating the arts into your healing journey

The arts have a unique way of tapping into our emotions and helping us connect with our deepest selves. For those who have lost touch with their Creator, incorporating the arts into your healing journey can be a powerful tool for renewing your communication with Him. In this subchapter, we will explore some techniques for incorporating the arts into your healing journey.

Artistic Bible Study Methods

One way to incorporate the arts into your healing journey is through artistic Bible study methods. This can include using art, music, or poetry to meditate on Scripture and gain a deeper understanding of God's word. For example, you might create a piece of art inspired by a particular passage, or write a poem based on a story from the Bible. These creative exercises can help you connect with God in a new and meaningful way.

Drama and Storytelling in Sermons

Another way to incorporate the arts into your healing journey is through drama and storytelling in sermons. Many churches now use drama and storytelling as a way to engage their congregation and bring the message of Scripture to life. These techniques can be especially powerful for those who struggle with traditional forms of worship, as they offer a more experiential and interactive way to connect with God.

Christian Mindfulness and Meditation

Christian mindfulness and meditation practices can also be a powerful tool for those seeking to renew their communication with God. These practices involve focusing on the present moment and becoming more aware of your thoughts, emotions, and physical sensations. By incorporating prayer and Scripture into your mindfulness and meditation practice, you can deepen your connection with God and experience a greater sense of peace and tranquility.

Writing and Journaling for Faith Exploration

Writing and journaling can also be powerful tools for exploring your faith and renewing your communication with God. By reflecting on your thoughts and experiences in writing, you can gain new insights into your relationship with God and deepen your understanding of His will for your life. This can be especially helpful for those who struggle to express themselves verbally or who find it difficult to connect with God in a more traditional way.

Healing Through the Arts

Finally, the arts can be a powerful tool for healing and transformation. Whether it's through music, art, or drama, the creative process can help us process our emotions and connect with our deepest selves. By incorporating the arts into your healing journey, you can tap into a powerful source of healing and renewal, and experience a greater sense of peace and wholeness.

The benefits of using the arts for healing

The benefits of using the arts for healing

The arts have always been a source of inspiration and comfort for human beings. From the earliest cave paintings to the most modern installations, the arts have helped us understand the world around us, connect with others, and express our deepest emotions. But did you know that the arts can also be a powerful tool for healing?

Research has shown that engaging in artistic activities can have a positive impact on our physical, emotional, and spiritual well-being. Here are just a few ways that the arts can be used for healing:

1. Reducing stress and anxiety: Creating art can be a meditative and calming experience, helping to reduce stress and anxiety. This is especially true for activities like drawing, painting, and coloring, which can be done in a quiet and peaceful environment.

2. Improving mood and self-esteem: Making art can also boost our mood and self-esteem by providing a sense of accomplishment and allowing us to express our unique perspectives and experiences.

3. Strengthening relationships: Participating in artistic activities with others can help us build stronger connections and foster a sense of community. This is particularly true for activities like group music-making, theater, and dance.

4. Enhancing spiritual growth: The arts can also be a powerful tool for exploring our faith and connecting with our Creator. Writing and journaling, for example, can help us reflect on our beliefs and experiences, while artistic Bible study methods can help us engage with scripture in new and meaningful ways.

5. Promoting physical healing: Finally, some forms of art therapy have been shown to have a positive impact on physical healing. For example, music therapy has been used to help patients manage pain and improve recovery after surgery.

Overall, the arts offer a unique and powerful way to connect with ourselves, others, and our Creator. Whether we are struggling with physical or emotional challenges, or simply looking to deepen our faith, incorporating artistic activities into our lives can help us find healing and renewal.

Conclusion

Recap of the importance of unlocking your creative spirit for renewed faith

Recap of the Importance of Unlocking Your Creative Spirit for Renewed Faith

As we journey through life, we often experience moments when we feel disconnected from our Creator. We may feel lost, uncertain, and overwhelmed by the challenges and pressures of daily life. However, one powerful way to renew our communication with God is by unlocking our creative spirit.

Right-Brained Christianity is a unique approach to faith that emphasizes creativity, imagination, and intuition. This approach recognizes that we are not just rational beings, but also emotional, spiritual, and creative beings. By tapping into our right-brain capacities, we can experience a deeper, richer, and more satisfying relationship with God.

Artistic Bible Study Methods are another powerful tool for unlocking our creative spirit. By using art, music, poetry, and other creative forms, we can engage with the Bible in a new and meaningful way. This approach allows us to see the Bible as a living, breathing text that speaks to us in our own language and context.

Drama and Storytelling in Sermons is another effective way to unlock our creative spirit. By using drama and storytelling, we can bring the Bible to life and make it relevant to our modern lives. This approach allows us to connect with the emotional and spiritual dimensions of the Bible and to see how it applies to our everyday struggles and challenges.

Christian Mindfulness and Meditation is another powerful tool for unlocking our creative spirit. By practicing mindfulness and meditation, we can quiet our minds and open our hearts to the presence of God. This approach allows us to experience a deep sense of peace and tranquility, and to connect with our Creator in a profound and transformative way.

Writing and Journaling for Faith Exploration is another effective way to unlock our creative spirit. By writing and journaling, we can explore our faith, our doubts, and our questions in a safe and supportive environment. This approach allows us to express our deepest thoughts and feelings, and to connect with our Creator on a personal and intimate level.

Healing Through the Arts is another powerful way to unlock our creative spirit. By engaging in art, music, dance, and other creative forms, we can heal our emotional and spiritual wounds, and find new meaning and purpose in our lives. This approach allows us to connect with our Creator in a profound and transformative way, and to experience the joy and beauty of life in all its richness and diversity.

In summary, unlocking our creative spirit is a powerful way to renew our communication with God. By tapping into our right-brain capacities, using artistic Bible study methods, engaging in drama and storytelling, practicing Christian mindfulness and meditation, writing and journaling for faith exploration, and healing through the arts, we can experience a deeper, richer, and more satisfying relationship with our Creator. So let us unlock our creative spirit and renew our faith today!

Final thoughts and encouragement for incorporating creativity into your spiritual life.

Final Thoughts and Encouragement for Incorporating Creativity into Your Spiritual Life

As we come to the end of this book, it is our hope that you have been inspired and equipped to incorporate creativity into your spiritual life. We have explored various right-brained Christian practices that can help you connect with God in new and meaningful ways. From artistic Bible study methods to drama and storytelling in sermons, from Christian mindfulness and meditation to writing and journaling for faith exploration, and from healing through the arts, we have shown how creativity can be a powerful tool for renewing your faith.

But incorporating creativity into your spiritual life is not just about learning new techniques or practices. It is about cultivating a mindset that values and embraces creativity as an integral part of your relationship with God. It is about recognizing that creativity is not just for artists or writers but is a fundamental aspect of being human. We were all created in the image of a creative God, and when we tap into our own creative potential, we are able to experience His presence and love in new and transformative ways.

So, as you continue on your spiritual journey, we encourage you to keep exploring and experimenting with different forms of creativity. Don't be afraid to try something new or to step outside of your comfort zone. Whether you are painting, dancing, journaling, or simply taking a walk in nature, allow yourself to be open to what God might be saying to you through these experiences.

Remember, creativity is not just a means to an end, but it is also an end in itself. Enjoy the process of creating and let yourself be surprised by what emerges. Trust that God is with you every step of the way, guiding you and inspiring you to new heights of creativity and spiritual growth.

In closing, we pray that this book has been a source of inspiration and encouragement for you on your journey towards a more creative and vibrant spiritual life. May you continue to unlock your creative spirit and discover new depths of love and intimacy with your Creator.

Insights

Feel free to write down any after-reading insights and thoughts

In 6 months from now I want to achieve...

-
-
-
-
-

9 798396 522473